HUDDERSFIELD TRAMWAYS
The original municipal system

Stephen Lockwood

Series editor Robert J Harley

This book is published to commemorate the 125th anniversary of the passing of the Huddersfield Corporation Act 1882, which empowered the Corporation to operate its own tramway system, being the first example of this concept in the United Kingdom.

Published February 2007

ISBN   *1 904474 95 0*
          978 1 904474 95 1

© *Middleton Press, 2007*

Design Deborah Esher

Published by
          Middleton Press
          Easebourne Lane
          Midhurst
          West Sussex
          GU29 9AZ
Tel: 01730 813169
Fax: 01730 812601
Email: info@middletonpress.co.uk
www.middletonpress.co.uk

Printed & bound by Biddles Ltd, Kings Lynn

CONTENTS

INTRODUCTION AND ACKNOWLEDGEMENTS

In 1983, all corporation buses around the country displayed a large circular sticker to commemorate one hundred years of municipal transport. The originator of this concept was a medium-sized town in West Yorkshire, whose operating territory was so difficult that privately owned companies could not be induced to lease and operate the newly constructed tramways.

This was by no means the only claim to fame of Huddersfield's tramway system. Such features as an unusual track gauge, a postbox service, and a coal-carrying operation all marked out the town's trams as being worthy of note. The routes themselves climbed hills as steep as 1 in 9, clung to the valley sides, and ran far beyond the Borough boundaries and even across the fields, into neighbouring settlements.

I lived in the town for the first twenty years or so of my life, until the early 1970s, and know that its citizens have long had a great interest in their local transport system. This was especially so in the days before 1974 when it was directly operated by the Corporation. The great affection which the trams enjoyed was transferred in equal measure to the replacing trolleybuses. This was reflected by the crowds of local people who literally lined the streets in July 1968 to see the last trolleybuses pass by, an experience which was denied to them when the last tram ran in 1940 because of wartime conditions.

Much of the available knowledge of the tramways is due to the efforts of two local residents. The late Bill Stocks created a photographic record of the last six years of operation and the changeover to trolleybuses. Information on the system was included in his book on local transport entitled 'Pennine Journey' published in 1958. Another local man, Roy Brook, the son of a tramway employee, began to make notes about the trams in his youth,

including the details of the many different types of top-covers. This developed into a serious and prolonged research into the tramway history. His first book on the subject appeared in 1959, and a subsequent and much expanded version, 'Huddersfield Corporation Tramways' appeared for the tramway centenary celebrations in 1983.

The purpose of this present volume is to complement previous works on the subject and to describe the system in pictures, taking the reader on a route-by-route electric tram ride.

My thanks go to the following individuals and organisations, without whose help the compilation of this book would have been impossible.

Roy Brook has read through my text and made suggestions and improvements where necessary. Huddersfield-born Peter Cardno, who has researched its motorbus history, has also read my text and commented accordingly as well as providing items from his collection. The Kirklees Image Archive, looked after by John Rumsey and Amanda Booth, has assisted by supplying many tramway images from its collection, not least examples from the Bill Stocks collection of which it is custodian. Prints from this archive can be purchased through their website: www. kirkleesimages.org.uk.

The maps have been drawn by Roger Smith, and are based on the ones prepared by him for the Light Railway Transit Association booklet on West Yorkshire Tramways.

Terry Russell has kindly supplied the excellent tramcar scale drawings.

Colin Barker, Stanley King and Geoffrey Smith have kindly allowed items from their collections to be used. Finally my appreciation goes once again to my wife Eileen, whose support and patience seems boundless.

GEOGRAPHICAL SETTING

Situated in the former West Riding of Yorkshire, Huddersfield is now part of the Metropolitan Borough of Kirklees. It lies in the foothills of the Pennines, and is seven miles from the neighbouring town of Halifax and eleven miles from the city of Bradford. Manchester lies 26 miles/41.8km across the Pennines in Lancashire. Huddersfield is founded on the trade and processing of wool, and its worsted cloth is world famous. Other notable industries are chemical and engineering, both of which were initially founded to support the woollen trade. The town became a Borough in 1868 and a County Borough in 1888. In 1883, its population was 81,000, which by 1940 had increased by over 50% to 125,000.

HISTORICAL BACKGROUND

The Huddersfield Improvement Act 1880 authorised the construction of 19 miles/30.5km of tram tracks to standard gauge, and a start was made to lay these. throughout the town. The actual width of the tracks was slightly less than authorised, being 4ft 7¾ins/1416mm, a dimension used elsewhere only on the tramways in Glasgow and Portsmouth, and which allowed standard gauge railway wagons to run on their flanges in the street. In practice this never happened in Huddersfield.

Having laid its tramways, the established practice was for the Corporation to lease the tracks to a tramway company, who would provide the cars and run the service. Despite extensive efforts, no such lessee was forthcoming, probably due to the adverse operating terrain with many steep and long hills (Chapel Hill, near the town centre was 1 in 11, the steepest gradient used by trams in England at the time). Undaunted, the Corporation applied for, and won, powers to operate its own tramways under the Huddersfield Corporation Tramways Act of 1882. Thus the concept of the 'Corporation Tram' was born.

The chosen method of traction was steam, comprising an engine hauling a passenger carrying double-deck trailer. Following a Board of Trade inspection in November 1882, the first service commenced between Fartown Bar and Lockwood Bar via the town centre, on 11th January 1883. The initial service was every hour, using one engine and car. There was an extension of track beyond Lockwood Bar along Meltham Road to Dungeon Wood to serve Beaumont Park and this was used sporadically at weekends and for special events. The same year saw a service introduced to Lindley via Trinity Street, followed in 1884 by services to Edgerton and Paddock Head. The former line was extended in 1886 via Holly Bank Road to meet the Lindley tracks, forming a circular route.

The next service to commence, in May 1885, was that to Moldgreen, which was routed in both directions via King Street in the town centre. It was considered unwise to operate steam trams in such a steep, narrow and busy thoroughfare, and accordingly horse traction was employed. This was a short lived operation and continued experience with steam operation led to the horse cars being replaced by their iron counterparts from March 1888. The final route opening of the decade came in 1889 when a service commenced to Almondbury.

Further powers authorising more routes were obtained in 1890. During the decade up to 1900, new services were inaugurated to Waterloo (an extension of the Moldgreen service) and Crosland Moor in 1890, to Leeds Road in 1891, to Birkby, Bradley, Berry Brow and Salendine Nook in 1892, to Newsome Road in 1896 and in 1899 to Outlane and Manchester Road (Borough boundary). A further extension to the line along Manchester Road, taking trams outside the Borough, became possible in May 1900, after Linthwaite UDC had laid three miles of track terminating at Slaithwaite (Star Inn), and leased this to Huddersfield Corporation. At the same time the Paddock route was extended to Longwood (Quarmby Clough).

In March 1893, Royal Mail letter boxes

began to be carried by the cars and a special fare of 1d was payable if the car was stopped especially to post a letter. This facility was continued almost throughout the life of the tramways, being withdrawn at the beginning of the Second World War. Another interesting development from 1896 was the transport of refuse. This was carried, using two specially constructed four wheel wagons, from the Corporation refuse plant at Longroyd Bridge to a tip just beyond the Waterloo terminus. Short track extensions were necessary at both ends. The service was not continued after steam tram operation finished.

By 1900, the steam tram system comprised about 26 passenger cars running over 23 miles/ 37km of route. However, tramway technology had moved on and electric propulsion was seen as the key to future growth. Neighbouring Halifax had opened its tramway system from the start with electric trams in 1898.

The Huddersfield municipality therefore decided to convert the tram routes to electric traction and built a power station and depot for 25 cars at Longroyd Bridge for the first stage of conversion. On 14th February 1901, the first electric trams ran on the route to Outlane and the circular service via Trinity Street or Edgerton to Lindley. On 18th February, the Crosland Moor and Slaithwaite routes followed, and the first phase was completed a few days later on 25th February with the conversion of the Longwood route.

The introduction of electric cars did not mean the end of steam tram development. On 2nd April 1901, an extension of the Fartown route to Ash Brow Road, Sheepridge was opened. This was followed the next day by a line via Kirkgate to Westgate which allowed steam trams from Waterloo and Almondbury to terminate in the town centre without uncoupling.

The second stage of electrification came in mid-1902 when between May and July, the remainder of the routes were given over to electric trams. The Berry Brow tramway was extended to Honley in June, using steam trams for twelve days only before the new electric cars were ready, and the last steam trams of all ran to Fartown sports ground on 21st June 1902. Even then the Bradley route was not ready and it lost its tram service altogether for a few weeks until 13th July. The line from Lockwood Bar to Dungeon Wood was not converted to electric traction and the rails were removed.

The steam trams served Huddersfield well. However, as well as being cumbersome to operate they were slow, noisy and dirty. Special track arrangements were provided at many of the termini so that the cars did not have to be uncoupled for the engine to run round the trailer. These included triangular reversers or, as at Bradley, a turning circle. To avoid turning movements in the town centre, most routes were linked together across the town, a feature that was not initially perpetuated with the electric trams. Frequencies were poor, typically every 30 minutes or more, although on the plus side the trailer cars carried a high number of passengers (two of the fleet could accommodate 94 passengers each) and, of necessity to protect passengers from smoke and soot, they were fully enclosed, unlike the replacement electric cars.

In October 1904 a unique service of carrying coal to three mills on the Outlane route commenced, using specially purchased motorised coal trucks.

From December 1905, some routes were joined together, on an experimental basis, to form a cross-town facility. Trams now ran from Honley to Sheepridge and from Longwood to Birkby. In 1907 most other routes followed suit.

The Tramways Department began motorbus operation in 1920, initially running feeder services to main points on tram routes, the first service running from Paddock Head (on the Dod Lea route) to Golcar. These routes were developed to many other rural areas around the town and in 1929 an arrangement was agreed with the LMS railway company to operate motorbus services as a joint venture, known as the Huddersfield Joint Omnibus Committee.

Route numbers were introduced and shown on the cars from 1918. From 1923 until the end of the trams, the numbers and services were as follows:-

1 Lindley to Waterloo
2 Newsome to St George's Square
3 Outlane to Waterloo
4 Marsden to Bradley
6 Crosland Moor to St George's Square
7 West Vale to Almondbury
8 Dod Lea to Birkby
9 Brighouse to Northumberland Street
10 Honley to Sheepridge

Route number 5 was never allocated. During the 1930s, when some new route-linkages were introduced, the original numbers were maintained. For instance, a tram on the Crosland Moor to Brighouse service introduced in 1933 showed route number 9 when proceeding to Brighouse and 6 when proceeding to Crosland Moor.

The zenith of Huddersfield's tramway development came in 1931 when the first of eight fully-enclosed luxury trams entered service, these being destined to have short lives in the town. The electric tramway system, having been continually developed and extended since 1901, was now at its greatest extent, with 140 cars working over 38 miles/61km of route.

The need to replace the track to Almondbury resulted in the Corporation deciding to experiment with a trolleybus service and replace the trams on this route. Trolleybuses commenced operation in December 1933, although the Almondbury trams had actually ended some months beforehand to allow for removal of the track. The success of the more 'flexible' trolleybus led to the closure and conversion to trolleybuses of all the tram routes over the next seven years.

The dates that the last trams ran on each route were as follows:-

Almondbury	16th April 1933
Outlane/Lindley to Waterloo	10th November 1934
Newsome	1st May 1937
Crosland Moor	2nd October 1937
Birkby	3rd October 1937
Marsden	9th April 1938
Bradley	20th April 1938 (to Deighton until 18th June 1938)
Sheepridge	18th June 1938
Dod Lea	25th September 1938
Honley	19th February 1939
West Vale	27th May 1939
Brighouse	29th June 1940

Due to the inability of trolleybuses to pass under the bridge in Woodhead Road at the end of Lockwood Viaduct, the Honley tram service was replaced by motorbuses of the Joint Omnibus Committee, trolleybuses running only as far as Lockwood Church.

Thus, Huddersfield's last tram, car 132, left Northumberland Street for Brighouse in the blackout of the Second World War, fifty seven years after the pioneering days of the first ever 'corporation tram' in January 1883.

Tramcar builder abbreviations used in the captions
BEC – British Electric Car Company
UEC – United Electric Car Company

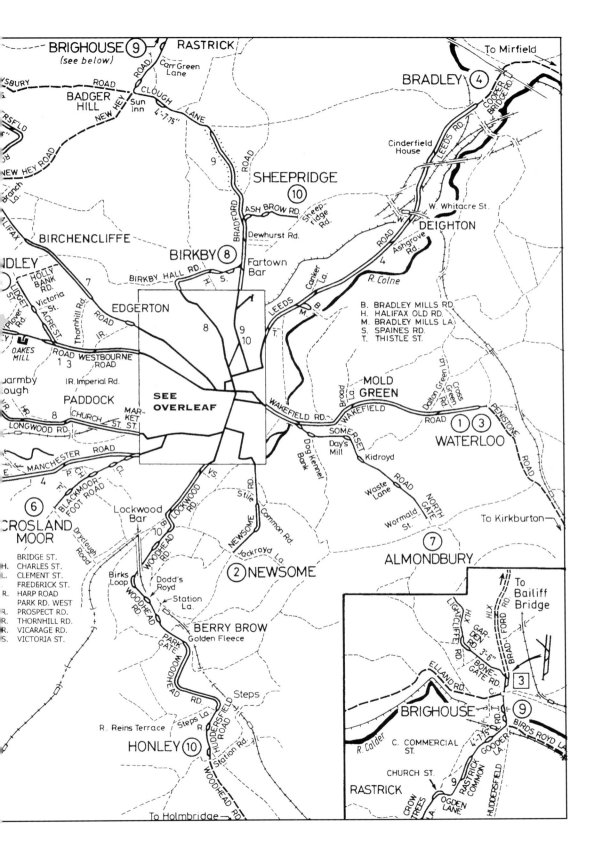

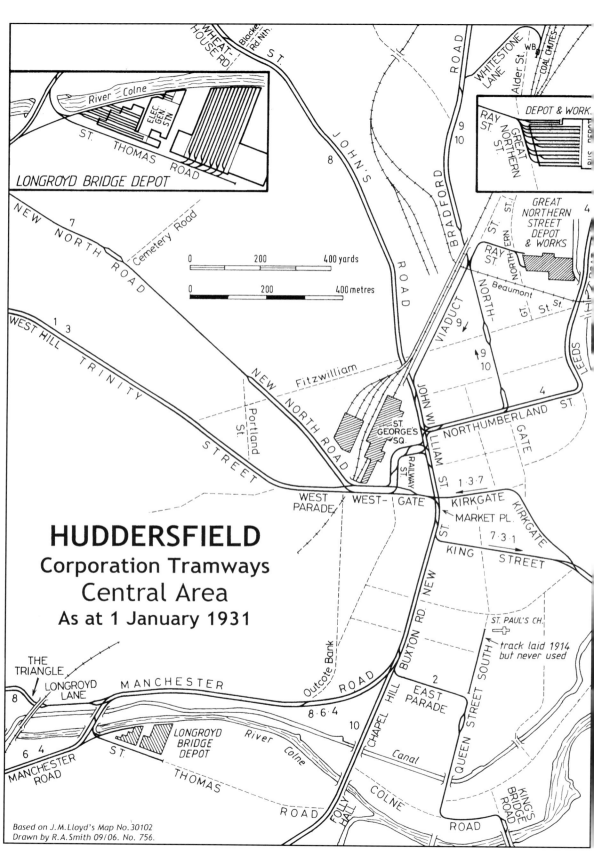

LONGROYD BRIDGE DEPOT

River Colne

ELEC GEN STN

ST. THOMAS ROAD

WHEAT-HOUSE RD.

Blackee Rd. Nth.

ST.

JOHN'S

8

ROAD

BRADFORD ROAD

9

10

WHITESTONE LANE

Alder St.

COAL CHUTES

WB

DEPOT & WORK

RAY ST.

GREAT NORTHERN ST.

NEW NORTH ROAD

7

Cemetery Road

0   200   400 yards

0   200   400 metres

1 3

WEST HILL

TRINITY

STREET

Portland St.

NEW NORTH ROAD

Fitzwilliam

St. St.

RAY ST.

NORTH-

GREAT NORTHERN STREET DEPOT & WORKS

4

Beaumont

St. St.

LEEDS

VIADUCT

9

9 10

NORTHUMBERLAND   ST.

GATE

4

JOHN WILLIAM ST.

ST. GEORGE'S SQ.

Railway St.

WEST PARADE

WEST- GATE

1·3·7

KIRKGATE

MARKET PL.

KIRKGATE

HUDDERSFIELD
Corporation Tramways
Central Area
As at 1 January 1931

NEW

KING   STREET

7·3·1

ST. PAUL'S CH.

track laid 1914
but never used

THE TRIANGLE

LONGROYD LANE

8

MANCHESTER

Outcote Bank

ROAD

BUXTON RD.

CHAPEL HILL

2

EAST PARADE

QUEEN STREET SOUTH

8·6·4

10

6 4

MANCHESTER ROAD

ST.

THOMAS

LONGROYD BRIDGE DEPOT

River Colne

ROAD

Canal

FOLLY HALL

COLNE

ROAD

KING'S BRIDGE ROAD

Based on J.M.Lloyd's Map No.30102
Drawn by R.A.Smith 09/06. No. 756.

HUDDERSFIELD CORPORATION TRAMWAYS.

DIAGRAM

SHOWING

TRAMCAR NUMERICAL AND MOTOR OMNIBUS ALPHABETICAL STAGES

DECEMBER 1923.

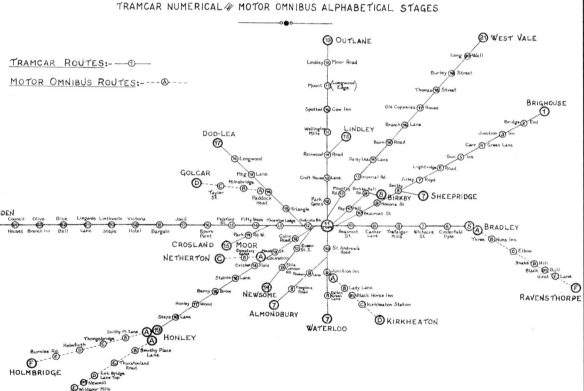

STEAM DAYS

1. A late 1880s view of Black Hawthorn engine no 9, dating from 1886, hauling an 1883 built Starbuck open top trailer seating 34. This trailer had already been modified with the fitting of bogies instead of the original four wheel truck. The location is Lockwood Bar.
(Kirklees Museums and Galleries K008792)

MILNSBRIDGE.

S. George's Square	Return
7 20	7 40
8 0	8 20
8 40	9 0
9 20	9 40
10 0	10 20
10 40	11 0
11 20	11 40
12 0	12 20
12 40	1 0
1 20	1 40
2 0	2 20
2 40	3 0
3 20	3 40
4 0	4 20
4 40	5 0
5 20	5 40
6 0	6 20
6 40	7 0
7 20	7 40
8 0	8 20
8 40	9 0
9 20	9 40
10 0	10 20
10 40	11 0

Inside 2d.
Outside 1½d.

1d. Stage (Inside) Longroyd Bridge.
1d. Stage (Outside) Birkhouse.

NEWSOME RD.

S. George's Square	Return
7 30	7 45
8 0	8 15
8 30	8 45
9 0	9 15
9 30	9 45
10 0	10 15
10 30	10 45
11 0	11 15
11 30	11 45
12 0	12 15
12 30	12 45
1 0	1 15
1 30	1 45
2 0	2 15
2 30	2 45
3 0	3 15
3 30	3 45
4 0	4 15
4 30	4 45
5 0	5 15
5 30	5 45
6 0	6 15
6 30	6 45
7 0	7 15
7 30	7 45
8 0	8 15
8 30	8 45
9 0	9 15
9 30	9 45
10 0	10 15
10 30	10 45
11 0	11 15

Inside 2d.
Outside 1d.

1d. (Inside) Corner of Colne Road and Queen Street South.

OUTLANE.

S. George's Square	Return
6 45	7 30
7 15	8 0
8 15	9 0
a8 45	a9 0
9 15	10 0
a9 45	a10 0
10 15	11 0
a10 45	a11 0
11 15	12 0
a11 45	a12 0
12 15	1 0
a12 45	a1 0
1 15	1 30
1 45	2 0
2 15	2 30
2 45	3 0
3 15	3 30
3 45	4 0
4 15	4 30
4 45	5 0
5 15	5 30
5 45	6 0
6 15	6 30
6 45	7 0
7 15	7 30
7 45	8 0
8 15	8 30
8 45	9 0
9 15	9 30
b9 45	b10 30
10 15	11 0
c10 45	c11 30

a Marsh only.
b Saturdays only.
c Salendine Nook only except on Saturdays.

Inside, 4d.
Outside, 3d.

(Inside) Vernon Avenue, Luck Lane or Bay Horse, Plover Road or Tanyard Lane and Salendine Nook.
(Outside) Luck Lane, Marsh, and Salendine Nook.

Huddersfield Corporation Tramways
TIME TABLE.

ALMONDBURY.

S. George's Square	Return
7 30	8 4
8 30	9 4
9 30	10 4
10 30	11 4
11 30	12 4
a12 0	12 34
12 30	1 4
1 0	1 34
1 30	2 4
2 0	2 34
2 30	3 4
3 0	3 34
3 30	4 4
4 0	4 34
4 30	5 4
5 0	5 34
5 30	6 4
6 0	6 34
6 30	7 4
7 0	7 34
7 30	8 4
8 0	8 34
8 30	9 4
a9 0	a9 34
a10 0	a10 34
10 30	11 4
a11 0	a11 34

a Saturdays only.

Inside, 3d.
Outside, 2d.

1d. (Inside) Somerset Road and Kidroyd Bridge.
1d. (Outside) Somerset Terrace.

BERRY BROW.

S. George's Square	Return
7 45	8 15
8 45	9 15
9 45	10 15
10 45	11 15
11 45	12 15
12 15	12 45
1 15	1 45
1 45	2 15
2 15	2 45
2 45	3 15
3 15	3 45
3 45	4 15
4 15	4 45
4 45	5 15
5 15	5 45
5 45	6 15
6 15	6 45
6 45	7 15
7 15	7 45
7 45	8 15
a8 15	a8 45
8 45	9 15
a9 15	a9 45
9 45	10 15
a10 15	a10 45
10 45	11 15

Passing Lockwood each way 15 minutes later.
a Tuesdays&Sat'days

Inside, 3d.
Outside, 2d.

1d. (Inside)Rashcliffe, Bridge-st. & Birks.
1d. (Outside) Bridge-st., Lockwood.

BRADLEY.

S. George's Square	Return
7 30	8 0
8 30	9 0
9 30	10 0
10 30	11 0
11 30	12 0
12 30	1 0
1 0	1 30
1 30	2 0
2 0	2 30
2 30	3 0
3 0	3 30
3 30	4 0
4 0	4 30
4 30	5 0
5 0	5 30
5 30	6 0
6 0	6 30
6 30	7 0
7 0	7 30
7 30	8 0
8 0	8 30
8 30	9 0
a9 0	a9 30
9 30	10 0
a10 0	a10 30
10 30	11 0
b11 0	b11 30

a Tuesdays&Sat'days
b Saturdays only.

Inside, 3d.
Outside, 2d.

1d. (Inside) Canker Lane & Whitacre-st.
1d. (Outside) Whitacre-st.

2.   The standard combination of steam tram in Huddersfield was the Kitson engine and enclosed Milnes bogie trailer. This scene is on the Birkby route on Spaines Road at the junction of Halifax Old Road. The cars on this route worked a circular service from the town centre via Bradford Road, returning via Birkby, then through the town to Lockwood. Frequencies were low – this service ran every 30 minutes. (Author's collection)

CROSLAND MOOR.

To — 7·0 7·40 8·20   9·0 9·40 10·20 11·0 11·40
     12·20 1·0 1·40 2·20   3·0 3·40 4·20 5·0
     5·40 6·20 7·0 7·40 8·20   9·0 9·40 10·20

From — 7·20 8·0 8·40 9·20 10·0 10·40 11·0
    12·0 12·40 1·20 2·0 2·40 3·20   4·0 4·40
    5·20 6·0 6·40 7·20 8·0 8·40 9·20 10·0
    10·40

FARES: Inside, 2d. Outside, 1½d.

1d. Stage : — Inside, Longroyd Bridge.
Do.   Outside, Birkhouse Lane.

Waterloo.

To — 7·0 8·0 9·0 10·0 11·0 12·0 1·0 2·0 3·0
    4·0 5·0 6·0 7·0 8·0 10·0 10·45

Passing Moldgreen terminus at a quarter past each hour

From — 7·30 8·30 9·30 10·30 11·30 12·30 1·30
    2·30 3·30 4·30 5·30 6·30 7·30 8·30 9·30
    10·30 11·10

Passing Moldgreen terminus at a quarter to each hour

Fares : From Huddersfield to Waterloo

Inside, 3d. Outside, 2d.

Between Moldgreen and Waterloo

Inside, 2d. Outside, 1d.

HUDDERSFIELD CORPORATION TRAMWAYS,
TIME TABLE. 1891/2
Lindley.

To Lindley (via Edgerton) — 7·15 7·45 8·15
    8·45 9·15 9·45 10·15 10·45 11·15 11·45 12·15
    12·45 1·15 1·45 2·15 2·45 3·15 3·45 4·15
    4·45 5·15 5·45 6·15 6·45 7·15 7·45 8·15
    8·45 9·15 9·45 10·15 10·45.

Passing Thornhill Road every hour and half-hour, from 7-30 a.m., to 11 p.m.

To Lindley (via Marsh) — 7·30 8·0 8·30
    9·0 9·30 10·0 10·30 11·0 11·30 12·0 12 30
    1·0 1·30 2·0 2·30 3·0 3·30 4·0 4·30
    5·0 5·30 6·0 6·30 7·0 7·30 8·0 8·30
    9·0 9·30 10·0 10·30.

Passing Wellfield Road at a quarter to and a quarter past every hour, from 7-45 a.m., to 10-45 p.m.

From Lindley (via Marsh) — 7·35 8·5 8·35
    9·5 9·35 10·5 10·35 11·5 11·35 12·5 12·35
    1·5 1·35 2·5 2·35 3·5 3·35 4·5 4·35
    5·5 5·35 6·5 6·35 7·5 7·35 8·5 8·35
    9·5 9·35 10·5 10·35 11·5

Passing Wellfield Road at a quarter to and a quarter past every hour from 7-45 a.m. to 10-45 p.m.

From Lindley (via Edgerton) — 7·50 8·20 8·50
    9·20 9·50 10·20 10·50 11·20 11·50 12·20 12·50
    1·20 1·50 2·20 2·50 3·20 3·50 4·20 4·50
    5·20 5·50 6·20 6·50 7·20 7·50 8·20 8·50
    9·20 9·50 10·20 10·50 Sat. 11·20

Passing Thornhill Road every hour, and half-hour from 7-30 a.m. to 11-0 p.m. Saturday 11-30

Fares : Inside, 3d. Outside, 2d.

1d. Inside Stages (via Marsh), Vernon Street & Wellfield Road
1d. do.   (via Edgerton), Cemetery Road & Thornhill Road
1d. Outside Stages do.   Sunnybank Road
1d. do.   (via Marsh) Luck Lane

3. This is John William Street in the 1890s, at the height of the steam tram era. In the foreground Kitson engine no 15 hauls a Milnes trailer en-route for Fartown. The car behind is bound for Lockwood. (Author's collection)

Huddersfield Corporation Tramways

1892

TIME TABLE.

PADDOCK.

40 Minutes' Service of Cars. (Red Lights.)

From St. George's Square at 7-20 8-0 8-40 9-20 10-0 10-40 11-20 12-0 12-40 1-20 2-0 2-40 3-20 4-0 4-40 5-20 6-0 6-40 7-20 8-0 8-40 9-20 10-0 10-40. Saturdays 11-0.
Returning from Paddock at 7-40 8-20 9-0 9-40 10-20 11-0 11-40 12-20 1-0 1-40 2-20 3-0 3-40 4-20 5-0 5-40 6-20 7-0 7-40 8-20 9-0 9-40 10-20 11-0. Saturdays 11-20

Through Fares: Inside, 2d. Outside, 1½d.

1d. Stages :—Inside, Longroyd Bridge ;
Outside, Brow Road.

SALENDINE NOOK.

Hourly Service of Cars. (White Lights.)

From St. George's Square to Salendine Nook at a quarter to each hour, from 7-45 a.m. to 10-45 p.m.
Passing Wellfield every hour from 8 a.m. to 11 p.m.
Returning from Salendine Nook at a quarter past each hour, from 8-15 a.m. to 11-15 p.m.
Passing Wellfield every hour from 8-30 a.m. to 11-30 p.m.

Through Fares : Inside, 3d. Outside, 2d.

1d. Stages :—Inside, Vernon Avenue, Bay Horse and Tanyard Lane ; Outside, Luck Lane, Marsh.
Double Service on Saturdays, commencing at 12-15.

WATERLOO.

Hourly Service of Cars. (White Lights.)

From St. George's Square every hour, from 7-0 p.m. to 10-0, and Saturdays, 11-0 p.m.
Passing Moldgreen at a quarter-past each hour.
Returning from Waterloo every hour, from 7-35 a.m. to 10-35 and 11-15 p.m., and Saturdays 11-20 p.m.
Passing Moldgreen at a quarter to each hour, from 7-45 a.m. to 10-45 & 11-20 p.m., and Sats., 11-30 p.m.

Through Fares : Inside, 3d. Outside, 2d.

1d. Stages :—Inside, Aspley, Moldgreen, and Dives House ; Outside, Moldgreen.
Double Service on Saturdays, commencing at 12-30.

ALMONDBURY.

Hourly Service of Cars. (White Lights.)

From St. George's Square to Almondbury, at half-past every hour from 7-30 a.m. to 10-30 p.m.

Returning from Almondbury at 8 minutes past every hour from 8-8 a.m. to 11-8 p.m.

Through Fares : Inside, 3d. Outside, 2d.

1d. Stages :—Inside Aspley and Kidroyd Bridge ; Outside, Somerset Terrace.

BERRY BROW.

Hourly Service of Cars. (Green Lights.)

From St. George's Square to Berry Brow at a quarter to each hour, from 7-45 a.m. to 10-45 p.m.
(Passing through Lockwood at every hour.)

Returning from Berry Brow at a quarter past each hour, from 8-15 a.m. to 11-15 p.m.
Passing through Lockwood at half-past each hour.

Through Fares : Inside, 3d. Outside, 2d.

1d. Stages :—Inside, Rashcliffe, Bridge Street, and Birks ; Outside, Bridge Street, Lockwood.

Double Service on Tuesdays and Saturdays, commencing at 12-15 noon.

BRADLEY.

Hourly Service of Cars. (White Lights.)

From St. George's Square to Bradley at half-past each hour, from 7-30 a.m. to 10-30 p.m. Saturdays 11-0.
Returning from Bradley each hour, from 8 a.m. to 11 p.m. Saturdays 11-30.

Through Fares : Inside, 3d. Outside, 2d.

1d. Stages :—Inside, Canker Lane & Whitacre Street. Outside, Whitacre Street.

Double Service Daily from 12 noon to 4. Saturdays, 11.

BRIGHOUSE

4.   From March 1923, the northernmost terminus of Huddersfield's tramway system was at
Brighouse, five miles from Huddersfield town centre. The trams reversed at the junction of
Huddersfield Road and Commercial Street, where car 119 is seen on a Sunday morning in April
1938. Stretching into the distance is Bradford Road, where two tram services of Halifax Corporation
(3ft 6ins/1067mm gauge) once operated, both terminating at the other side of this junction. One of
these ran to Halifax via Hipperholme until 1931. The other lasted only until 1929, and ran along
Bradford Road to Bailiff Bridge, where it met the 4ft/1219mm gauge trams of Bradford Corporation.
Thus, between 1923 and 1929, there was almost a continuous line of tramway from Huddersfield
to Bradford, although three different track gauges were involved. Huddersfield's Brighouse service
was service 9, and for a brief period in 1938, the Sunday morning service was operated as a through
service to Marsden, a 12 mile run, hence the route number shown on the car.
(WA Camwell / National Tramway Museum)

←————— 5.   Huddersfield Road Brighouse is seen here in the very early months of the Second World War. Due to a dispute with the railway company regarding the use of trolleybuses over the bridge at Brighouse Station, the tram service had a brief stay of execution and survived into the summer of 1940. A tram can be seen at the terminus in the distance, whilst the trolleybus overhead is erected and ready for use. A sign on the left hand traction pole reads 'Trolley Vehicles Stop Here'. The Albert cinema on the left survived until 1970. (Author's collection)

←————— 6.   Just beyond Brighouse town centre, the route turned off the main Huddersfield Road into Gooder Lane towards Rastrick. The trams crossed the railway at Brighouse Station, and this bridge was at the centre of the dispute between Huddersfield Corporation and the LMS Railway Company, who were concerned about the weight of two trolleybuses crossing on the bridge as opposed to a single track tramway. The argument was eventually settled with the Corporation agreeing to supply spare traction poles to be used to provide additional support for the bridge structure. This view shows Sunbeam trolleybus 582 crossing the bridge in 1953. These vehicles had a relatively short life on this service, the route being cut back to the Borough boundary at Fixby in 1955. Note that the road paving still shows evidence of the former tram track, and also the compulsory stop marked on the traction pole on the left. (Roy Brook)

7.   From Brighouse, the track was single with passing loops as far as the tramroad at Fixby. This is Gooder Lane looking towards Brighouse from the top of a tramcar waiting in the loop for English Electric car 121 to pass. The trolleybus wiring is in process of erection in this 1939 view.
(AD Packer)

8.   This delightful mid-1920s view of Rastrick Common, looks towards Huddersfield, and shows the single track. The tram in view is BEC car 42, which had just been rebuilt in the Corporation's own workshops into a fully enclosed car, outwardly resembling the latest batch of English Electric cars. (Author's collection)

9.   At the Sun Inn, the route turned sharp left into Clough Lane towards Fixby and Huddersfield. This view shows the first day of operation, on Monday 12th March 1923. UEC car 78, decorated overall and carrying the legend 'Success to Brighouse – Huddersfield' on its sides, is operating a special service between this point and Brighouse (see also photograph 112). The track and wires curving into Clough Lane can be seen on the right.
(Kirklees Museums and Galleries K004043)

10.   At Fixby, the route crossed the Borough boundary into Hudderfield. Here, a three-quarter mile stretch of reserved sleeper track tramroad took the line southwards towards Fartown. At the Bradley Lane entrance to the tramroad the single track from Brighouse became double. The entrance to the single track was protected by a small semaphore indicator on an adjacent traction pole worked by the passage of the car's trolley over a skate in the overhead wire. These signals were used elsewhere on the system on single line sections where the loop was not visible from the next one. This view was taken on the last day of tramway operation, Saturday 29th June 1940, shows a car entering the tramroad bound for Huddersfield. Note the temporary wooden spacer bars placed in the overhead wiring to keep the new trolleybus wires clear of the tram wires. (Roy Brook)

←————— 14. A view showing the rural nature of the tramroad. It features car 109 near the southern end starting the climb to Fixby. This is another wartime view. (Author's collection)

←————— 15. Balcony car 117 negotiates the reverse curves at the southern end of the tramroad and will shortly emerge onto Netheroyd Hill Road behind the New Inn. It is working on the through service to Crosland Moor and therefore displaying route number 6. Initially, the Brighouse service worked to and from the town centre only, terminating at the top of Northumberland Street (see photograph 73). From 1933 until 1937, the service was linked as a through run to Crosland Moor, then to Honley until 1939, before reverting to terminating in the town centre.
(WB Stocks / Kirklees Museums and Galleries K020077)

16.   Smithy junction, Fartown, where Ashbrow Road joins Bradford Road, was the point at which the Brighouse and Sheepridge route diverged. The track junction is seen here with Ashbrow Road on the right. Enclosed English Electric car 130 is passing balcony car 114. Car 130 was latterly unique in having built-in side destination boxes over the platform, a feature just visible in this view.
(HB Priestley / National Tramway Museum)

SHEEPRIDGE

17.   The Sheepridge terminus was situated at the end of Ashbrow Road, at its junction with Woodhouse Hill, which runs behind the tram in this view. The route was extended from Fartown Bar using steam trams in 1901, becoming electrically operated a year later. BEC canopied car 68 is seen with its crew. This car was rebuilt in 1924, becoming fully enclosed with direct stairs. (Author's collection)

→ 18.   When the Sheepridge tram service was replaced by trolleybuses in June 1938, these vehicles turned right at the end of Ashbrow Road to return to Fartown Bar via Woodhouse Hill and vice-versa as a circular route via Fartown Green.   Part of Woodhouse Hill had a gradient of 1 in 8.3, steeper than on any of the tram routes. In 1949, the trolleybus circular route was abandoned, being replaced by separate routes operating into the council estates at Brackenhall and Riddings. Thus the eastern part of Ashbrow Road lost its transport service entirely.   This 1960 scene shows Karrier trolleybus 501 climbing Woodhouse Hill en route to Riddings passing the former tram terminus. (CW Routh)

→ 19.   Having converged at Smithy junction (see photograph 16), the Sheepridge and Brighouse routes ran via Bradford Road into the town centre. This very typical late 1930s Huddersfield roadscape shows Bradford Road between Smithy and Fartown Bar, looking north. The junction with Richmond Avenue is on the left. The road is paved with stone setts and the trolleybus wiring is already in place. The former tram poles have been retained, with an additional metal crosspiece linking both poles forming a gantry, thus giving the added strength necessary to support the extra weight. In the middle distance, at the junction with Dewhurst Road, was a

crossover which was used to reverse trams terminating at Fartown. In April 1934, Sunday morning services were introduced for the first time in Huddersfield, and a consequence of this was that the Brighouse trams, which at that time ran through to Crosland Moor, were routed via Birkby for these few hours each week. To gain the Birkby tracks at Fartown Bar, the cars reversed on this crossover then ran 'wrong line' on the outbound track to Fartown Bar where there was a direct connection into Spaines Road. This avoided the need for passengers having to reverse their seats at Fartown Bar. (WE Turton / Kirklees Museums and Galleries K019787)

20.   Fartown Bar was where the Bradford Road and Birkby tracks connected, the Birkby service terminus being a few yards away along Spaines Road. These connecting tracks were mainly used for rugby football special cars to the Fartown ground at Spaines Road, which worked from town via the Birkby Route, then turned right at Fartown Bar to return to town via Bradford Road. When the Birkby service was converted to trolleybus operation in 1937, there were not enough trolleys to operate the football specials, so trams were still used on match days, but operating via Bradford Road only and reversing at the Dewhurst Road crossover. This scene shows football special trams congregating at Fartown Bar, with the fans seen on the right commencing the short walk up Spaines Road to the ground. The leading enclosed car on the right is a service car for Sheepridge. Note the remarkable full circle of wiring erected for the trolleybuses, which was used by Birkby service vehicles to turn round. The trams retained their own set of wires through this circle, as can be seen here. (WB Stocks / Kirklees Museums and Galleries K020126)

21.   The original track layout south of Fartown Bar towards town was single track with passing loops. In 1924, this part of Bradford Road was widened, allowing for double track to be laid. This is an early view of the original single track in Bradford Road, Hillhouse looking north. Eleanor Street is on the left. In the distance a tram with 'Magrini' top cover is seen at the Honoria Street loop. (Author's collection)

22.   At the town end of Bradford Road the double track became single where the trams passed under the viaduct carrying the railway to Dewsbury and Leeds. Immediately after negotiating the viaduct, there was a track junction allowing Brighouse trams to turn right into Viaduct Street, which formed part of the one way turning loop for the service. There was also the connection to and from the lower part of Viaduct Street, which led via Ray Street to Great Northern Street depot and works. Sheepridge trams carried straight on and used Northgate in both directions. Following the demise of the Birkby trams in 1937, the Viaduct Street track became disused and Brighouse trams used Northgate in both directions, reversing at the top of Northumberland Street. In this view from 1938, English Electric car 112 is proceeding to Brighouse, and the severed connections into Viaduct Street can be seen in the left foreground. In the distance, enclosed English Electric car 130 is waiting at the end of the double track in Bradford Road to proceed under the viaduct towards town. (HB Priestley / National Tramway Museum)

23.   Looking in the opposite direction to the previous photograph, this view shows Huddersfield's other street tramway, the Gas Works railway. This was a steam-worked goods tramway opened in 1922 which linked the former Midland Railway goods yard at Newtown, off St John's Road, with the Corporation gas works in Leeds Road. The line was authorised under the Huddersfield Corporation General Powers Act 1920, which also authorised the Brighouse route including the tramroad at Fixby. The gas works line, was standard gauge and crossed the passenger tramway at two points. It left Newtown goods yard, passing under the railway viaduct and immediately crossed the junction of Viaduct Street and Northgate. It then proceeded along the full length of Beaumont Street (near to Great Northern Street tram depot) and crossed the Bradley route tramway at Leeds Road into the gasworks. Two Peckett 0-4-0 saddle tank steam locomotives worked the line, which closed in 1966. Engine no 2, by then under the ownership of the North Eastern Gas Board, is seen in 1953 crossing Viaduct Street and Northgate, having just emerged from under the viaduct pulling a train of coal wagons. Flagmen walked in front of the train on the street section. Note the trolleybus wiring and the Hebble bus on the jointly operated bus service between Huddersfield and Bradford, which commenced in 1928.
(Huddersfield Examiner / Kirklees Museums and Galleries Ke 23562)

BIRKBY

24.　　The Birkby route terminus, seen here, was in Spaines Road adjacent to Fartown Bar, and there were track connections to and from Bradford Road (see photograph 20). The lefthand overhead wire behind BEC car 65 curves round to the right, this being the connection used by the football special cars returning to town from the Rugby League ground, situated in Spaines Road. The wire on which the car's trolley pole is placed is connected to the northbound wire in Bradford Road, towards Sheepridge or Brighouse. Although most termini outside the town centre were provided with trolley reversers by the 1920s, this one, together with those at Bradley and West Vale, never had one. Presumably this was because at these particular points, trams started from the terminus on an uphill slope. The normal service from here was route 8 through to Dod Lea or Longwood, a linking made as early as 1905 and never subsequently altered throughout the life of the Birkby trams. This car is probably working on a rush hour special duty.
(HB Priestley / National Tramway Museum)

25.　The terminal track loop at Birkby was in the eastern part of Wasp Nest Road, this part being later incorporated into Spaines Road. This was a favourite spot for enterprising photographers to take images of the trams with their crews. This example shows Milnes car 18, which was later to receive a BEC Wilkinson type top cover in 1914. (Author's collection)

26.　The middle portion of the Birkby route comprising Birkby Hall Road and Norman Avenue (which was later incorporated into Birkby Hall Road) was quite spectacular, with a sharp downgrade followed by an equally sharp upgrade, known locally as the 'switchback'. This pleasant Edwardian suburban scene shows Milnes car 11 climbing the 1 in 12 gradient of the 'switchback' on its way via the town centre to Longwood. It will turn sharply into Wheathouse Road as indicated by the rails in the foreground. (P Cardno collection)

27.   At Blacker Road, where the Birkby trams crossed from Wheathouse Road into St John's Road, there was a crossover which cars used regularly at rush-hours, serving Hopkinson's valve works.   This is a very early view, which may even predate the establishment of Hopkinson's Britannia Works in 1904.   It shows a well laden Milnes bogie car in St John's Road, just having crossed Blacker Road.   The side board on the tram reads 'Fartown Circle', which was the short lived original routeing of the Birkby electric cars, operating from town via Bradford Road to Fartown Bar then back via Birkby and vice-versa. (Author's collection)

28.   This is St John's Road, looking towards Wheathouse Road with Blacker Road running across the view in the middle distance.   In the background is Hopkinson's Britannia Works.   A canopied BEC car with 'Bailey' top cover is seen proceeding towards Birkby. By mid-1908, double track existed between this point and the town centre. (Author's collection)

BRADLEY

29.   The Bradley terminus was at the junction with Leeds Road and Bradley Lane, where a typical passenger shelter was provided. Milnes bogie car 12 poses for the photographer in this view in the early days of electric traction. In the background can be seen Cooper Bridge station on the railway embankment which carried the Lancashire and Yorkshire Railway main line from Wakefield to Manchester via Halifax. The station closed in 1960.
(Kirklees Museums and Galleries K002283)

30.   This scene shows the tram accident at Bradley which took place on Easter Saturday 22nd April 1905. Car 24, with Magrini top cover and still fitted with bogies, ran away from a point outside the Woodman Inn, some distance before the terminus, and derailed at the end of the track ending up in the grounds of Bradley Villa. The conductor was slightly hurt. The event was recorded by a local photographer. (Author's collection)

31.   Leeds Road was a heavily industrialised area, and the wool and chemical industries predominated. The crossover at Whitacre Street, shown as Deighton on tram indicators, served the adjacent LB Holliday chemical plant. In the final months of the Leeds Road trams, from April 1938, the service was cut back to this point and a motorbus shuttle service provided to and from Bradley connecting with the trams. This was because there were two railway over-bridges between here and the terminus which were too low for trolleybus operation and therefore needed to be altered. The disused Midland line railway bridge was removed entirely. The bridge in the background to this photograph, which carried the Kirkburton branch railway, had the roadway lowered under it to provide increased headroom. This view shows car 94 reversing at Deighton during this period. Note also the typical police box on the right-hand side. In Huddersfield these were painted red and some survived well into the 1960s.
(WB Stocks / Kirklees Museums and Galleries K020104)

32.   The last extension to the Huddersfield tram system was opened in August 1923 and comprised of a loop off Leeds Road around Bradley Mills Lane and Bradley Mills Road, adjacent to the Huddersfield Town Football Club's Leeds Road ground. At this time the team was one of the most successful in the country and on match days a procession of trams conveyed fans to and from the ground. This scene at the end of a match shows the crowds engulfing a variety of cars waiting to take them to the town centre. (WB Stocks / Kirklees Museums and Galleries K011241)

33.   The Bradley trams entered the town centre from Leeds Road via Northumberland Street. Seen crossing Northgate is UEC car 83 shortly before the service was converted to trolleybuses. From April 1938, the Bradley route was linked with that to Longwood, hence the route number 8 being displayed. The trolleybuses used Northumberland Street in the town direction only, and Bradley bound vehicles ran via Brook Street and Union Street. In this view the new trolleybus overhead is in place, with a temporary tram wire remaining for trams to Bradley. The trolleybus overhead curving round from the left was part of the connection for trolleys entering service from Great Northern Street depot, and this was also used by the Sheepridge and Brighouse trams. (WB Stocks / Kirklees Museums and Galleries K020116)

WATERLOO

34.   The Waterloo Hotel was the terminus of the tram route which took its name, and the Hotel is still situated on Wakefield Road, where Penistone Road branches off to the right in this view. In the 1920s, UEC car 95 is at the terminus on the Outlane service. The trolley reverser can be seen in front of the car. (Kirklees Museums and Galleries K002706)

									BIRKBY and DOD LEA.	Route No. 8.
8	**BIRKBY**									
9	1d.	**BIRKBY HALL ROAD**								
10	1d.	1d.	**BAY HALL**							
11	1½d.	1d.	1d.	**JOHN WILLIAM STREET** (queue)						
12	2d.	1½d.	1d.	1d.	**OUTCOTE BANK**					
13	2½d.	2d.	1½d.	1d.	1d.	**TRIANGLE**				
14	3d.	2½d.	2d.	1½d.	1d.	1d.	**PADDOCK HEAD**			
15	3½d.	3d.	2½d.	2d.	1½d.	1d.	1d.	**MEG LANE**		
16	4d.	3½d.	3d.	2½d.	2d.	1½d.	1d.	1d.	**LONGWOOD OLD TERMINUS**	
17	4d.	4d.	3½d.	3d.	2½d.	2d.	1½d.	1d.	1d.	**DOD LEA**

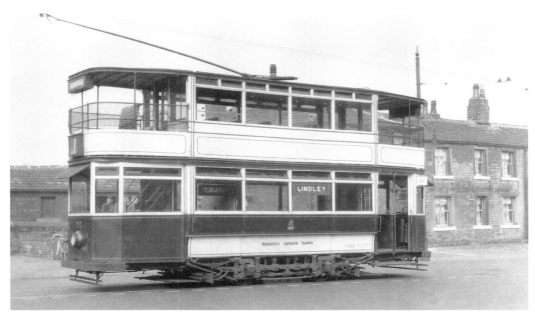

35.   A closer view of the terminus shows, showing UEC car 75 waiting to depart for Lindley in the early 1930s. (Dr H Nicol / National Tramway Museum)

HUDDERSFIELD CORPORATION TRAMWAYS.

ALTERATION OF
SUNDAY TIME TABLE.

On and after January 5th, 1902, the Cars will be run as follows :-

ELECTRIC CARS.

CROSLAND MOOR		OUTLANE.		LINDLEY Via Marsh		LINDLEY Via Edgerton		LONGWOOD		1 LINTHWAITE			
St. George's Square	Return	St. George's Square	Return	St. George's Square	Return	St. George's Square	Return	St. George's Square	Return	St. George's Square	Return	St. George's Square	Return
1 45	2 0	2 0	2 40	2 20	2 40	1 50	2 10	2 0	2 30	1 40	2 20	6 0	6 40
2 15	2 30	3 0	3 20	3 0	3 20	2 30	2 50	2 30	3 0	2 0	2 40	6 20	7 0
2 45	3 0	3 20	1 0	3 40	4 0	3 10	3 30	3 0	3 30	2 20	3 0	6 40	7 20
3 15	3 30	4 0	4 40	4 20	4 40	3 50	4 10	3 30	4 0	2 40	3 20	7 0	7 40
3 45	4 0	4 40	5 20	5 0	5 20	4 30	4 50	4 0	4 30	3 0	3 40	7 20	8 0
4 15	4 30	5 20	6 0	5 40	6 0	5 10	5 30	4 30	5 0	3 20	4 0	7 40	8 20
4 45	5 0	6 0	6 40	6 20	6 40	5 50	6 10	5 0	5 30	3 40	4 20	8 0	8 40
5 15	5 30	6 40	7 20	7 0	7 20	6 30	6 50	5 30	6 0	4 0	1 0	8 20	9 0
5 45	6 0	7 20	8 0	7 40	8 0	7 10	7 30	6 0	6 30	4 20	8 40	9 0	9 20
6 15	6 30	8 0	8 40	8 20	8 40	7 50	8 10	6 30	7 0	4 40	9 20	9 40	9 40
6 45	7 0	8 40	9 20	9 0	9 20	8 30	8 50	7 0	7 30	5 0	9 20	10 0	10 20
7 15	7 30	9 20	10 0	9 40	10 0	9 10	9 30	7 30	8 0	5 20	6 0	*10 0	*10 30
7 45	8 0	*10 0	*10 30			9 50	10 10	8 0	8 30	5 40	6 20		
8 15	8 30							8 30	9 0				
8 45	9 0	*Salendine Nook only						9 0	9 30				
9 15	9 30							9 30	10 0	*Bar Gate			
9 45	10 0							10 0	10 30				

ALMONDBURY

36. Almondbury is a village older than Huddersfield itself. The trams terminated in Northgate at the junction with Wormald Street, about two hundred yards from the parish church. BEC car 31, one of only two with full length canopies and lower deck 'Tudor Arch' windows, poses with its crew. Note the post box on the rear dash panel. The tram post service commenced in steam tram days and all cars carried them until the late 1930s, near the end of the system. The boxes were emptied periodically by Post Office staff in the town centre. (Author's collection)

37. The trams reached Almondbury from Wakefield Road via Somerset Road. At the foot of the climb to the village, opposite Dog Kennel Bank, is BEC car 64, one of the 'Chivers Jelly' trams, an early example of all-over advertising. Even the stair risers advertise Chivers products.
(Author's collection)

NEWSOME

38.   Newsome terminus was at the top of Newsome Road at Newsome Church, a climb of 1 in 9.5 from the bridge over the River Colne at King's Mill. The service was extended to this point from Stile Common Road in July 1911. The Board of Trade imposed restrictions due to the severe gradient and insisted that the new section was constructed as double track. The Newsome service was never linked to another route and always operated as a shuttle to St George's Square. This 1920s scene shows BEC car 56 with the conductor standing on the rear platform.
(Author's collection)

39.   This is the scene at the bottom of Newsome Road on 3rd March 1906 when Milnes car 26 ran away and derailed, coming to rest against the side of building. BEC car 35 has been brought in to tow the car back onto the rails. Following this incident, car 26 eventually re-entered service with its Magrini top cover replaced by a unique design of home built 'Bailey' cover which had a balcony roof at each end. From this point, the Newsome route entered the town centre by way of Colne Road, Queen Street South and East Parade (see photograph 83). (Author's collection)

48.   The domed roof English Electric cars delivered in 1931-1932 were regular performers on the Marsden to Bradley service. Car 144, the highest numbered tram in the fleet, has just arrived at Marsden terminus and the conductor has already hooked the bamboo pole onto the car's trolley pole ready to turn it for the return journey. Normally, this action would not have been necessary because of the automatic trolley reverser, but trolleybus wiring is in place and the reverser has been removed. (Author's collection)

49.   The portion of the Marsden route from the Huddersfield boundary at Spurn Point to Slaithwaite was originally owned by Linthwaite Urban District Council. This created disputes between the two authorities as to the adequate maintenance of the track. It was eventually purchased by Huddersfield in 1910. This is a view of the original electric tram terminus at the 'Star Hotel' Slaithwaite showing Milnes bogie car 21 with Magrini top cover. (Roy Brook collection)

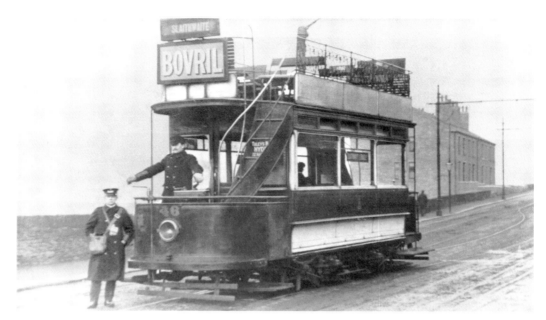

50.　A study of uncanopied BEC car 46 on Manchester Road bound for Slaithwaite after 1907.
It is near Norman Grove, Linthwaite and the Royal Oak. This car subsequently received a BEC
'Wilkinson' top cover and in 1925 became one of the first cars in the fleet to be scrapped.
(Author's collection)

51.　The Marsden service joined the Crosland Moor tracks from Blackmoorfoot Road at the
Griffin Inn on Manchester Road, a short distance beyond Longroyd Bridge. English Electric car
119 is seen on a damp day having just negotiated the junction en route to Marsden, although by
this time (1938), the Crosland Moor trams had been converted to trolleybuses, whose wires can be
seen trailing in behind the car. The bridge in the background carries the railway to Penistone via
Berry Brow and Honley. See also photograph 54. (WA Camwell / National Tramway Museum)

DOD LEA AND LONGWOOD

52.   This is leafy Dod Lea terminus, which was the third and final terminus of the tram service in this area. The original electric tram ran as far as the west end of Quarmby Clough, and the line was extended into Longwood village as far as the Rose and Crown Inn in 1904. In March 1920, the route was further extended through the village to the western edge at Dod Lea. This view shows rebuilt Milnes car 12 waiting to depart for Birkby (shown on the side indicator), the through service being introduced in 1905. (Dr H Nicol / National Tramway Museum)

53.   Between Longwood and Paddock, the route took the tortuous road around the valley side at Quarmby Clough, which until 1904 had been the terminus of the route. This scene on the Paddock side of Quarmby Clough is looking from the open balcony of a BEC car, with an English Electric car approaching and showing Longwood village in the background with Longwood Tower on the hillside above the tram. Conversion of the route to trolleybuses is imminent, as can be seen by the overhead wiring. (WB Stocks / Kirklees Museums and Galleries K020154)

54. At Longroyd Bridge, the Dod Lea route branched off from the Crosland Moor and Marsden services close to the depot. English Electric car 112 is entering the stretch of single track along Longroyd Lane on the last day of the Dod Lea tram service, 25th September 1938. On the other side of the wall beside the tram is the Huddersfield Narrow Canal, which crossed into Lancashire by means of the Standedge canal tunnel beyond Marsden. The railway viaduct carried the Lancashire and Yorkshire Railway branches to Penistone, Holmfirth and Meltham. (WB Stocks / Kirklees Museums and Galleries K020112)

OUTLANE

55. The tram terminus at Outlane was one of the highest in the country at 909 feet above sea level. Until 1905, the trams terminated at Stainland Road. The introduction of the coal tram service to Gosport Mills, some 200 yards beyond the terminus in October of that year resulted in the passenger service being extended to the point where the tracks left the road into the Mill premises. However, the deteriorating condition of this extension (which was laid with secondhand rails) led to the passenger service reverting to the old terminus between 1916 and 1925, when the relaying of this section led to its reinstatement. This is the general scene of the terminus with UEC car 75 ready to return to town. Behind the car is the trolley reverser which will automatically reverse the trolley when the car sets off. The track used by the coal trams curves round to the left of this view. (Authors collection)

56. This photograph records the first outing of a new domed roof English Electric car on 21st August 1931. On this occasion, car 138 took members of the Corporation's Tramways committee to Outlane, where they transferred onto a new AEC Regal bus of the Huddersfield Joint Omnibus Committee. This would take them to 'Nont Sarah's', a popular hostelry on the moors towards Lancashire, where the party would take lunch. Note the track curving into Gosport Mills in the bottom foreground. (Roy Brook collection)

──────→ 57. The Outlane route was almost a continuous climb from the town centre. In 1915, the track between Salendine Nook and the original Outlane terminus was doubled. Here, UEC car 78 is climbing from Salendine Nook towards Mount just after these works were completed. (Roy Brook collection)

──────→ 58. This lovely portrait shows Milnes car 1 in near original condition including bogies. It is standing in New Hey Road at the 'Bay Horse' junction, Marsh, where the Outlane and Lindley routes diverged. The view looks towards town and the Lindley tracks pass behind the gas lamp on the left of the photograph. (D Broadbent collection)

LINDLEY

59. From the 'Bay Horse' junction, the Lindley route ran in almost a straight line via Acre Street and Lidget Street. The tram terminus, seen here, was at the junction with Holly Bank Road, where a standard Huddersfield waiting shelter was provided. In the early days of the electric trams, there was a service beyond this point via Holly Bank Road to connect with the Edgerton service at Halifax Road, this facility being withdrawn in 1911 when the Halifax Road service was extended to Birchencliffe (see photographs 68 and 69). In this scene, BEC car 27, with 'Tudor Arch' lower–deck windows is at Lindley terminus before turning into Holly Bank Road, via the track evident in the foreground. Car 27 was one of only two 'Tudor Arch' cars with a full length canopy and reversed stairs. (Roy Brook collection)

→ 60. Another look at Lindley terminus in the early electric days. BEC car 65, with Magrini top cover, pauses before turning into Holly Bank Road to return to town via Edgerton. The lack of advertisements on the car indicates that it was almost brand new when the photograph was taken. The tram shelters of this style have, with two exceptions, long gone. One at Imperial Road, Edgerton on the former West Vale tram route survives today, being the only example existing in the town, and has thus served the travelling public for over 100 years. Another, which was formerly located at the junction of Norman Avenue and Halifax Old Road on the Birkby route until the 1970s, was dismantled for preservation and re-erected at the Sandtoft Trolleybus Museum near Doncaster, where it can still be seen. (Author's collection)

→ 61. This view of Acre Street, Lindley, looks towards Lidget Street and the tram terminus. In the distance is the Lindley Clock Tower, completed in Art Nouveau style in 1902. Enclosed English Electric car 132, later to become Huddersfield's last tram, is approaching on the Waterloo service. (Author's collection)

WEST VALE

62. Huddersfield's trams reached the settlement of West Vale, which was nearer Halifax than Huddersfield, when the track was extended from Elland in May 1914. The terminus, shown here, was in Saddleworth Road. A few yards further west was the junction with Stainland Road, where, until 1934, Halifax's trams (3ft 6ins/1067mm gauge) ran through the village to Stainland. In the distance can be seen the railway viaduct, carrying the Stainland branch from Halifax which ran in direct competition with the trams until 1929. BEC car 33 is at the terminus in 1932, and a Halifax tram can be seen in the background travelling towards Halifax. (Author's collection)

→ 63. Looking in the opposite direction, rebuilt BEC car 61 waits at the terminus before departing for Huddersfield and Almondbury. The conductor is sitting on the front step of the car. (Author's collection)

→ 64. Between West Vale and Elland, the tramway ran along Long Wall at Hullen Edge, where the road clung to a ledge overlooking the Calder Valley. Sensibly, the track was laid on the inside edge of the roadway as can be seen here with car 109 approaching West Vale from Elland. The passing loop was the last one before the terminus. Note the new trolleybus wiring coming in from the left – this was the end of the one way loop around West Vale necessary to allow the trolleybuses to turn. Interestingly the trolleybus terminus was in Stainland Road, once used by Halifax Corporation trams. (WB Stocks / Kirklees Museums and Galleries K020124)

65.   The largest centre of population on the West Vale route was the town of Elland, where UEC car 92 is seen at the junction of Victoria Street and Southgate. The trams were extended to this point in January 1914. The prominent building on the right is Elland Town Hall, which was being used as a cinema, showing 'talkies'. (WB Stocks / Kirklees Museums and Galleries K020076)

66.   The route out of Elland to Huddersfield included the steep climb up the Ainleys, which included two sharp bends. Nearing Ainley Top on the climb from Elland is English Electric car 103, just before it passes under the first of two high road bridges. In the background is the view over Elland. (HB Priestley / National Tramway Museum)

67.   This is Halifax Road, Birchencliffe at the junction with Burn Road on the climb from the town centre to Ainley Top. Car 112 is en route to West Vale on the last day of service, 27th May 1939. Note the fare stage sign on the left-hand traction pole. Numbered fare stages were introduced in the early 1920s, and Burn Lane was fare stage 15.
(WB Stocks / Kirklees Museums and Galleries K011242)

HOLLY BANK ROAD

68.   The original working of the Lindley tram service was as a circular service operating to Lindley via New North Road and Edgerton, or via Trinity Street and Marsh, the two sections being linked at Lindley via Holly Bank Road. In 1907, when several cross town routes were created, the Edgerton service ran through to Almondbury. Both Lindley services had different frequencies so it seems that the circular service ceased at this time and each element was worked as a separate route with a common terminus at Lindley. In 1911, the Edgerton tramway was extended along Halifax Road to Birchencliffe and the Holly Bank Road line was abandoned. The incident depicted here occurred in June 1905, when car 67 ran away in Holly Bank Road and left the rails at the junction of Halifax Road, ending up in a field. This car was a second hand purchase, previously being an exhibition car. It is believed to have been built in America (see Rolling Stock section). The four window body with thick surrounds was unique in the fleet.

(Author's collection)

69.   Following the abandonment of the service along Holly Bank Road, the track connections at each end of the road were severed. The track along the road itself, however, remained in situ until after the Second World War. This is a view of the disused track seen from the Halifax Road end. (WB Stocks / Kirklees Museums and Galleries K020119)

AROUND THE TOWN CENTRE

70.   One of the main focal points of Huddersfield town centre is St George's Square. The splendour of the Square has greeted travellers emerging from the railway station since the mid-nineteenth century. It is dominated by the George Hotel, seen on the left, which dates from 1850. The trams used the Square as part of a link between the north-south routes in John William Street, and the east-west routes in Westgate. Spare cars, or those awaiting their next duty, were often stored here and this practice carried on into trolleybus days. Note the ornate traction poles and the trolleybus turning circle crossing through the tram wires. This is an early 1938 scene showing Karrier trolleybus no 56 in the centre and an open balcony tram on service 10 passing along John William Street.(Commercial postcard / Author's collection)

71.   This view of St George's Square, taken in April 1938, looking westwards from the Tramways offices and showing the famous railway station building in the right background. Parked in the centre is English Electric car 108 beside a Karrier trolleybus. (Roy Brook collection)

72.   The northern part of John William Street is seen here, together with the railway bridge leading into St John's Road on the Birkby route. This was the only route to use this part of the street until the Brighouse service opened in 1923. These cars used the single line in Viaduct Street (previously used by cars operating from Great Northern Street depot) as a terminal loop, turning directly into Northumberland Street. This view of an UEC car en route to Birkby dates from between 1912 and 1914. The fenced off ground at the top of Brook Street was later the site of the Empire Cinema which opened in 1915. Note also the railway station water tower on the left, a structure that still exists. (Roy Brook collection)

73.   The Bradford Road and Bradley services left the town centre via Northumberland Street, which was opposite St George's Square. The Tramway offices were located at the top of this street, on the corner with John William Street and the Brighouse trams terminated here. This 1920s view shows an uncanopied BEC car waiting to depart for Brighouse, a regular type of car on this service. (Author's collection)

74.   A special service of tramcars operated from Northumberland Street on match days to the Huddersfield Town football ground on Leeds Road (see photograph 32). These were worked by any spare trams which were available, usually the older cars. Both the trams shown here, dealing with the long queue are fully enclosed rebuilt BEC cars, with no 61 in the rear. Note the sign on the left which states 'Queue here for cars to the football match Leeds Road'. (WB Stocks / Kirklees Museums and Galleries K020113)

75. This busy scene is in John William Street alongside St George's Square. The Newsome and Crosland Moor cars terminated here as shown by English Electric car 101 in the process of having its trolley turned. On the right an enclosed English Electric car can be seen turning into Northumberland Street. (WB Stocks / Kirklees Museums and Galleries K020103)

76.   Winter in John William Street. This is a dramatic view of English Electric car 110 keeping the tram service going in difficult conditions. Some of the older Milnes and BEC cars were equipped with wooden snow ploughs to clear the tracks.
(WB Stocks / Kirklees Museums and Galleries K020127)

←———— 77.　Car 67 is seen in John William Street in 1933 whilst operating a peak hour working to Trafalgar Mills. This was a point on the Bradley route and cars reversed at the Ashgrove Road crossover, some distance beyond the mills and adjacent to the British Dyes works. The car was, by this time, the only uncanopied car in the fleet with a 'Bailey' type top cover. Note domed roof car 141 in the background on a Dod Lea working.
(MJ O'Connor / AD Packer collection)

←———— 78.　At the Market Place, the single track of the Waterloo and Almondbury services, running from Kirkgate into Westgate, crossed the double track of the north-south services running from John William Street into New Street and vice-versa. All trams coming down Westgate turned right into New Street, and then resumed their eastward journeys via King Street. This view, taken about 1928, shows the junction of John William Street and Kirkgate. On the left, Milnes car 21 is waiting to cross into New Street on a Lockwood working, whilst in Kirkgate, an enclosed English Electric car bound for Lindley, is ready to cross into Westgate followed by a vestibuled BEC car for West Vale. Note the prominent Burton's store on the corner of John William Street. A McDonald's restaurant is now situated here.
(WE Turton / Kirklees Museums and Galleries K019909)

79.　Looking north along New Street towards the Market Place, this early view has captured BEC car 37 bound for Moldgreen and Waterloo turning into King Street. In the early days of electric traction, King Street was wired for use in both directions but was only used for eastbound cars. There was also a running wire curving left out of King Street into New Street although no equivalent trackwork existed.
(Roy Brook collection)

←——— 80. BEC car 63 with Magrini top cover is seen in this view looking down King Street from New Street. The Market Hall building can be seen further down the street on the right. When the Waterloo trams were replaced by trolleybuses in 1934, they were routed via Kirkgate and a recently constructed road known as Southgate. After that King Street lost its public transport service. (Author's collection)

←——— 81. This is a very early scene in the life of the electric tramway, showing the southern half of New Street. Milnes bogie car 3 is arriving in the town centre on a journey from Slaithwaite. Note the 'Workmens car' board stored beside the staircase for display on those journeys when workmens fares were available. The Imperial Hotel, across the street from Imperial Arcade, is prominent on the right. Car 3 achieved notoriety during its first days in service in 1901 by becoming the first car to traverse the lower part of Westgate even before any rails were laid there! On a journey from Lindley via Edgerton it ran out of control, failed to take the curve into Railway Street, and ended up in Westgate. Fortunately there were no serious injuries. (Author's collection)

82. Domed roof car 139 is seen gliding along New Street towards Chapel Hill on an August day in 1933. Collinson's Café is just visible behind the car.
(MJ O'Connor /
AD Packer collection)

83. At the southern end of Buxton Road (now absorbed into New Street), several tram routes diverged. The Marsden, Crosland Moor and Longwood trams bore right into Manchester Road. Those on the Honley service carried straight on down Chapel Hill towards Lockwood whilst the Newsome cars turned left into East Parade. Coming from Newsome, the trams performed an awkward manoeuvre dictated by the track layout which only allowed access to the outbound track in Buxton Road. Inbound trams therefore ran some yards 'wrong line' before regaining the correct track via the crossover in Buxton Road. UEC car 81 is seen turning out of East Parade onto the outbound track in Buxton Road. (WB Stocks / Kirklees Museums and Galleries K020169)

84. Tram service no 4 passengers have a choice of car in this scene on Manchester Road just beyond the junction with Chapel Hill, which descends to the right. BEC car 64, with its wooden seats, is leading domed roof car 143 which has deep cushioned seats. In the background is a Newsome car at the top of East Parade. The modern building in the background is the new extension to Huddersfield Co-operative Society's department store. This photograph is dated Saturday 1st May 1937, the last day of the Newsome service.
(HB Priestley / National Tramway Museum)

85. Returning to the Market Place crossing, this view of Kirkgate from Westgate shows how the double track in Westgate became single for the crossing, with a turnout into New Street. All trams coming down Westgate used this turnout. In this 1930s view, UEC car 80 is waiting at the traffic lights to cross from Kirkgate into Westgate on an Outlane working, followed by a BEC car.
(SL Smith)

86.   This is Westgate looking east at the junction with Market Street (on the right) and Railway Street (on the left). BEC car 34 approaches on a journey to Lindley via Edgerton and Holly Bank Road. The prominent building on the corner of Railway Street is the Ramsden Estate office. The Estate owned most of the land in Huddersfield until 1920 when it was purchased by the Corporation. (Author's collection)

87.   This scene, in the closing stages of the system, shows Westgate at the same point as the previous view. English Electric car 110 is waiting at the traffic lights having arrived from the West Vale direction. It will turn left into Railway Street to terminate adjacent to St George's Square. This had been the terminus for this route since 1933, when the through service to Almondbury was severed. (WB Stocks / Kirklees Museums and Galleries K020128)

COAL TRANSPORT

88. In October 1904, the Tramways Department inaugurated the operation of a coal delivery service to local mills using two specially constructed coal trams. These were built by GC Milnes Voss and Co and numbered 71 and 72. Three mills took part in the scheme, all situated on the Outlane route. Two were at Oakes (Wellington Mill and Oakes Mill) and special sidings were provided into the mill yards for the trams to discharge their cargo of 10 tons of coal. The third location (Gosport Mill) was beyond the outer end of the Outlane terminus and an extension using secondhand rails was constructed to the mill. Coal tram 72 (later re-numbered to 2) is seen in original condition demonstrating the unloading procedure at Wellington Mill. The view was probably taken on the special demonstration run in September 1904, attended by members of the technical press. (Author's collection)

89.　The coal was loaded at the Hillhouse railway yard coal chutes, and track was laid from Bradford Road along Whitestone Lane and across Alder Street into the yard. This is a closeup view of a coal tram loading at the coal chutes, showing the car in its final form with central trolley tower, (previously situated at one end of the car), and the replacement truck with the standard Spencer slipper brake. The narrowness of the platform is evident, this being due to the position of the chutes allocated to Wellington Mills, which were at the very end of the yard against the retaining wall. (Author's collection)

90.　This later view of one of the coal trams features it unloading at one of the mills. Note the trolley standard derived from a former open topped car. The service continued until 1934 (although the service to Gosport Mill ceased in 1926), when the imminent conversion of the Outlane route to trolleybus operation caused the demise of this unique piece of municipal enterprise. (Author's collection)

DEPOTS

91.   Originally, the steam engines and cars were temporarily housed in a wooden shed in Lord Street and then on an adjacent site in Northumberland Street that was later to become the Post Office. A permanent depot and works in Great Northern Street was opened in 1887. There was one entrance at the north-western corner of the building and trams ran to the depot from Northgate via Viaduct Street and Ray Street. In order to accommodate the growing number of cars in the fleet, the building was enlarged in 1909, when the western side became the main frontage, with eight entry doors topped with the wording 'Tramway Depot' in stone, and again in 1911 when the capacity was increased to 98 cars. By 1921 a new depot was constructed at Longroyd Bridge to house all the operational fleet and Great Northern Street depot's role became that of the works, overhauling the fleet and carrying out heavy repairs. The trolleybus conversion programme saw the return of all the remaining trams in 1938 until the system's closure. This view of English Electric balcony car 108 shows the 1909 frontage. Originally the doorways were rounded at the top, but difficulties with the clearance for trolleybuses caused the squaring off of the openings in 1934. The insulators in the overhead were due to the trolleybus wiring into each opening. These vehicles had to reverse out and transfer the booms to the wires in the street that this tram is using. (AD Packer)

92.   The first depot for the electric tram fleet was at Longroyd Bridge, near the junction of the Longwood and Crosland Moor routes. It adjoined the tramway power station and housed 25 cars. The growth of the electric tramway system meant that this building could not accommodate any additional cars, and these had to be housed at Great Northern Street. Subsequent increases in the fleet and enlargement of the latter premises meant that the 1901 Longroyd Bridge facility was not used for operational purposes between 1909 and 1914. After this date, the older cars, used on peak hour and football duties, were housed here until the site was incorporated into the new trolleybus depot in 1938. This scene dated 1933 shows BEC car 50 on the right with Milnes car 10 on the left. Both carry BEC Wilkinson type top covers. Note the proximity of the building to the River Colne, seen in the left hand corner of this view. (Dr H Nicol / National Tramway Museum)

93.   In July, 1921, a new depot was opened at Longroyd Bridge, adjacent to the 1901 car shed. The new facility accommodated 100 cars on 13 roads which were accessed from St Thomas Road. Thus the whole running fleet could be housed at Longroyd Bridge. This is a view of the westernmost bays of the 1921 depot in the latter part of 1937, showing car 135 on the right. Note the practice of hanging the car's bamboo trolley pole from the trolley head when parked in the depot. Huddersfield cars never carried trolley ropes and swivel trolley heads were used. The other cars in view had all been withdrawn from service in May and July 1937. Behind car 90 are cars 8, 93 and 95. On the extreme left are cars 48 and 10, some of the last unvestibuled cars to survive. Car 48 is evidently in the process of being dismantled. (HB Priestley/National Tramway Museum)

94.   These are the easterly bays of the 1921 depot, photographed on 28th August 1937 with UEC car 75 in view. Following the conversion of the Marsden tram service to trolleybuses in April 1938, these vehicles began to be housed in Longroyd Bridge depot for the first time. This was a temporary arrangement, as work was underway to convert the 1901 and 1921 depots into one building to house the entire trolleybus fleet. The remaining trams left Longroyd Bridge in November 1938 and were then housed at Great Northern Street. The side wall of the 1921 depot seen here became the back wall of the new trolleybus depot. (Author's collection)

ROLLING STOCK

Huddersfield's electric tram fleet can be split into three groups.

1. The Milnes and BEC cars built between 1901 and 1903 to replace the steam trams. Fleet numbers 1 to 70.

2. The UEC and English Electric cars built between 1909 and 1924 for extensions to the system. The final ten of these cars were totally enclosed. Fleet numbers 71 to 136

3. The English Electric domed roof 'luxury' cars built in 1931 and 1932 to allow for increased frequencies to services. Fleet numbers 137 to 144. The Milnes and BEC cars had complicated lives and most of these cars were considerably altered as follows:

Trucks

After initial experiments, all these cars ran with either Brill 21E or Mountain and Gibson 21EM trucks, replacing the Brill bogies on the first 25 cars and the BEC SB60 trucks on the remainder.

Track Brakes

The initial operating experience on the very hilly terrain of Huddersfield's tram routes was that the braking of the trams was inadequate. There was a spate of runaways, some of which have been pictured in earlier pages of this book. From 1910 onwards, after trying several designs, all cars were standardised on the CH Spencer slipper track brake to supplement the hand and rheostatic brakes; thereafter there were no serious incidents involving runaway trams.

Top covers

Only after a short time in service, it was realised that the open topped electric trams were inferior to the steam trams in one respect – the non-existent protection from the often hostile Pennine weather for top deck passengers. Thus in 1902, the cars began to be fitted with top covers, and eventually three types were used.

Magrini

The Magrini cover, named after the patentee, Bonomo Magrini, was an ingenious construction which was designed to fold away into the sides of the tram when not required (ie in good weather). For this reason the covers were labelled 'collapsible' and the trolley standard mounted on to the car's upper deck was retained, the pole poking out of a hole in the roof. 24 covers of this type were constructed by Milnes, Voss of Birkenhead and fitted to uncanopied cars. The upper deck windows matched the type of car the cover was placed on, the Milnes cars with this cover having five windows. The first car fitted was BEC car 49 in 1902 and it was soon evident that the covers were far too flimsy for Huddersfield operating conditions. All were replaced by 'Bailey' type covers around 1906. The cars known to have carried the Magrini covers were:- 8, 9, 15, 19, 21, 24, 26, 28 to 30, 40(ii), 43, 44, 45, 47, 49, 52, 54, 55, 56, 63, 64, 65, 66

Bailey

In 1905 car 70, the final BEC car, was fitted with a home-built permanent cover. This was similar to the 'Bailey' covers used in neighbouring Bradford. The design included a short saloon on the top deck of either three or four windows with the trolley mounted on the roof of the cover. 42 cars, canopied and uncanopied, received this type of cover in 1906-7, and there were several detail differences between individual cars. The cars were:- 7, 8, 9, 12, 14, 15, 19, 21, 23, 24, 25, 26 to 31, 33, 37, 39 to 45, 47, 49, 52, 54 to 57, 62 to 70.

Wilkinson

In 1912, the Huddersfield General Manager, RH Wilkinson designed a permanent top cover for uncanopied cars and 19 of these were supplied by UEC, five being mounted on BEC cars in 1912 and a further fourteen being supplied in 1914 to cover all the remaining open top Milnes cars. The covers were very well made and unlike the 'Bailey' type, they covered the whole of the top deck. The cars with 'Wilkinson' covers were:- 1 to 6, 10, 11, 13, 16, 17, 18, 20, 22 (1914), 46, 48, 50, 51 and 53 (1912). Car 30 subsequently carried the cover from 46. *(see photograph 102)*

95. **1 to 25**   **Milnes bogie cars**

The first electric trams for Huddersfield were
built by GF Milnes and Co of Hadley, Shropshire
and this 1900 view shows some of the cars being
built. (Author's collection)

HUDDERSFIELD CORPORATION ELECTRIC TRANWAYS.

HUDDERSFIELD CORPORATION ELECTRIC TRANWAYS.

Car 67 *(see photographs 68 and 77)*

This car, bought in 1903, was a 'one-off' of uncertain origin but is believed to have been built in the USA by the American Car Co of St Louis. Its design was identical to that of a batch of trams built by this manufacturer for the Dublin United Tramways Company and was possibly an exhibition car for the British Thomson-Houston Company who supplied the electrical equipment. The car was fitted with a Bailey type top cover around 1906. It remained in this condition throughout its life, and by the early 1930s was the only uncanopied car with this type of cover. It was withdrawn in 1933.

100. BEC cars – Magrini top cover

The first Huddersfield tram to carry a top cover was car 49 which received this 'Magrini' collapsible cover in late 1902. A total of 24 Milnes and BEC cars, all uncanopied, are known to have carried this type of cover including BEC cars 40(ii) and 63 to 66 which were fitted with these covers before entering service in 1903. The design was short lived due to their flimsy construction and all the cars had them replaced by home built Bailey type covers in 1906-7. Car 49 is seen after initial modifications, including the provision of a wooden door at the top of the stairs instead of a roller shutter. All subsequent covers of this type had a small window inserted above the destination board.
(Roy Brook collection)

101. BEC cars – Bailey top cover

The unsuitability of the Magrini covers resulted in these being replaced by the home constructed Bailey type, all except 13 of the BEC cars eventually receiving versions of this cover between 1905 and 1907. Both canopied and uncanopied cars were so treated. At the end of the 1920s and early 1930s those cars that had not been scrapped or otherwise rebuilt were given platform vestibules, necessitating extended roofs on the uncanopied cars. This is a view of uncanopied car 55 reversing at St George's Square during the 1920s, before being canopied and vestibuled. The last BEC cars were withdrawn in September 1938. (Author's collection)

102. BEC cars – Wilkinson top cover

Five uncanopied BEC cars which remained open-topped in 1912 received this new style of top-cover. Designed by the General Manager RH Wilkinson they were built by the United Electric Car Co (UEC). A sixth cover, which was all-enclosed, was fitted to canopied car 61 (see photograph 63 and caption under photograph 104). These covers were very durable, and when car 46 was scrapped

in 1925, its 'Wilkinson' cover was transferred to car 30, whose own 'Bailey' type was scrapped. Thus this car became the only one in the fleet to have carried all three types of top cover during its lifetime. This is car 30 seen in John William Street in 1933 on a rush-hour short working to Deighton (Whitacre Street). No cars with this type of cover (apart from car 61) were ever canopied or vestibuled. (MJ O'Connor)

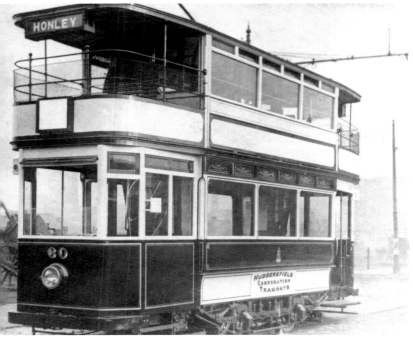

103. BEC rebuild – open-balcony car

Open top car 60 was given a thorough re-build in Great Northern Street works. In 1920 and emerged as a three window version of the latest English Electric cars with top cover and open balconies. The reversed stairs were replaced with the direct turn type. This car remained unique and was withdrawn in September 1938. It is seen in Ray Street before entering service in its new guise. (Roy Brook collection)

104. BEC rebuilds - totally enclosed cars

Three of the BEC cars, 42, 61 and 68 were eventually operated as all-enclosed cars. Car 61, which hitherto had never carried a top cover, was given an all enclosed top cover built by UEC in 1912, but retained its reversed stairs, eventually becoming all-enclosed in the late 1920s (see photograph 62). Cars 42 and 68 were rebuilt in Great Northern Street works in 1924 to resemble the newly deliv-

ered English Electric cars. They had their reversed stairs replaced by the direct turn type and angular dashes under the vestibules. Rebuilt car 68 is seen in John William Street in September 1938 about ten days before it was withdrawn from service. Both the other cars were withdrawn in the same year. (MJ O'Connor)

105. **1 and 2   Coal trucks**

Two motorised coal trucks were delivered in 1904 to operate the coal delivery service to three mills on the Outlane route. Built by Milnes, Voss of Birkenhead, these cars had the capacity to carry 10 tons of coal. The driver's platforms were very narrow due to the restricted space in the coal yard at Hillhouse. Their fleet numbers were 71 and 72, although they were renumbered 1 and 2 in their own series when the UEC cars were delivered in 1909. Originally mounted on Brush radial Lycett and Conaty trucks, the cars later received the standard Huddersfield 21E type. Both survived until the end of the coal delivery service in May 1934. Truck 2 is seen in its latter condition, including semi-circular headboards behind the driver and a trolley standard which had come from an open top passenger car. It is seen here having just departed from the Hillhouse coal chutes and is crossing Alder Street into Whitestone Lane with another load of coal.
(Roy Brook collection)

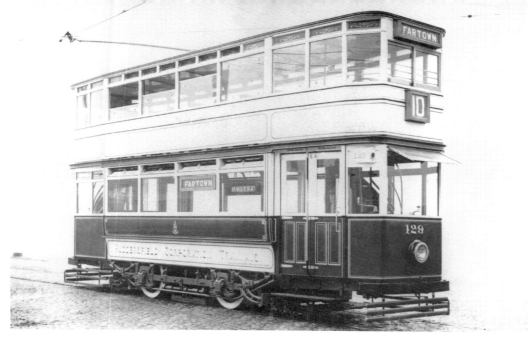

110. **137 to 144 English Electric domed roof cars**

These eight cars were delivered in 1931 (137 to 142) and 1932 (143, 144) and were the last trams bought. Of English Electric construction, they were of modern design with domed roofs, all enclosed bodies and a revised livery of Post Office red and cream. There were 58 upholstered seats, (62 in the later pair which had slightly longer bodies). The trucks were built by Maley and Taunton to their swing-link design. Air track brakes were fitted, being the first and only Huddersfield cars to have this feature. Contemporary trade literature was highly impressed with these cars. Initially, due to their superior speed compared with older cars, the batch was used on the Marsden to Bradley route and was always associated with this service, although they did regularly see use on other routes. All were sold to Sunderland Corporation in April 1938 following the conversion of the Marsden route to trolleybuses (see photographs 118 and 119). The first of these cars, 137 is seen posed in Great Northern Street when new. The final two cars had four ventilators instead of two on the between-decks panel and the other cars were subsequently altered to conform. (Author's collection)

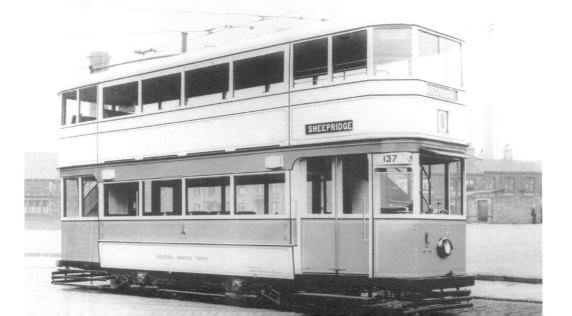

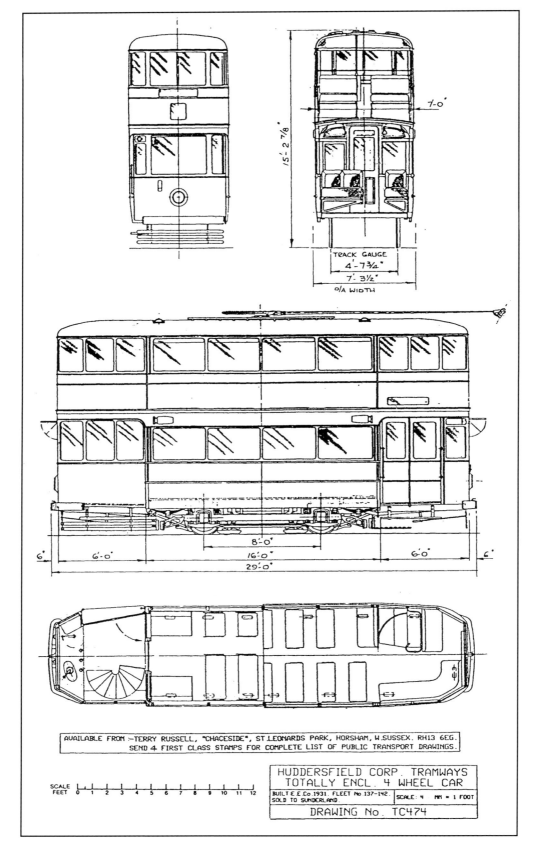

15'- 2 7/8"

7'-0"

TRACK GAUGE
4'- 7¾"
7'- 3½"
O/A WIDTH

8'-0"

16'-0"

29'-0"

6" 6'-0" 6'-0" 6"

AVAILABLE FROM :—TERRY RUSSELL, "CHACESIDE", ST.LEONARDS PARK, HORSHAM, W.SUSSEX. RH13 6EG.
SEND 4 FIRST CLASS STAMPS FOR COMPLETE LIST OF PUBLIC TRANSPORT DRAWINGS.

SCALE
FEET 0 1 2 3 4 5 6 7 8 9 10 11 12

HUDDERSFIELD CORP. TRAMWAYS
TOTALLY ENCL. 4 WHEEL CAR

BUILT E.E.Co.1931. FLEET No.137-142.
SOLD TO SUNDERLAND.

SCALE: 4 MM = 1 FOOT

DRAWING No. TC474

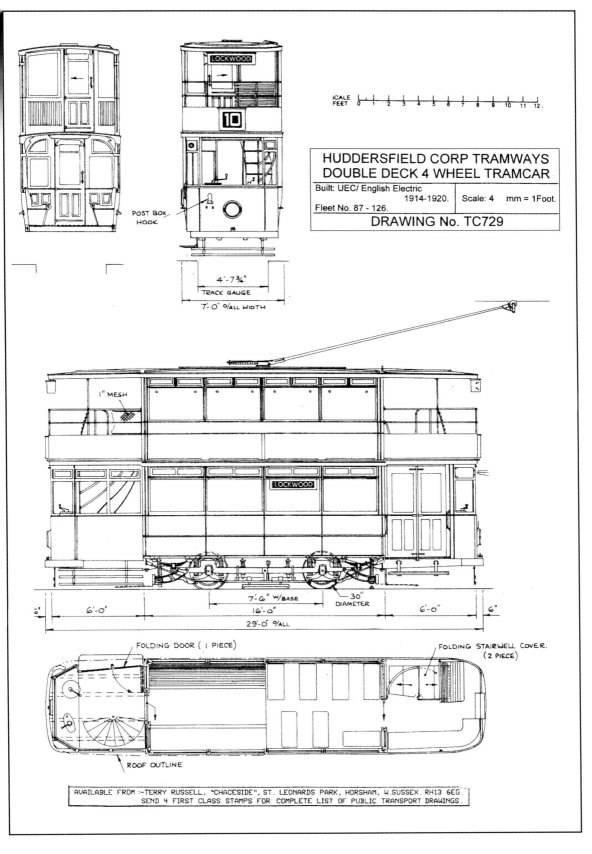

LOCKWOOD

10

iCALE
FEET 0 1 2 3 4 5 6 7 8 9 10 11 12

POST BOX
HOOK

HUDDERSFIELD CORP TRAMWAYS
DOUBLE DECK 4 WHEEL TRAMCAR

Built: UEC/ English Electric
1914-1920.   Scale: 4   mm = 1Foot.
Fleet No. 87 - 126.

DRAWING No. TC729

4'-7¾"
TRACK GAUGE

7'- 0" ⁰/ALL WIDTH

1" MESH

LOCKWOOD

7'-6" W/BASE

16'-0"

30"
DIAMETER

6'-0"

6"

0'

6'-0"

29'-0" ⁰/ALL

FOLDING DOOR (1 PIECE)

FOLDING STAIRWELL COVER.
(2 PIECE)

ROOF OUTLINE

AVAILABLE FROM :-TERRY RUSSELL, "CHACESIDE", ST. LEONARDS PARK, HORSHAM, W.SUSSEX. RH13 6EG.
SEND 4 FIRST CLASS STAMPS FOR COMPLETE LIST OF PUBLIC TRANSPORT DRAWINGS.

ALL DRESSED UP

111. To celebrate national and local events, an electric car would be suitably decorated and illuminated externally with coloured lamps. This would tour the system and provide a memorable spectacle. The first such occasion was for the Coronation of Edward VII in 1902. This unidentified Milnes car is dressed to celebrate an achievement of the Huddersfield Rugby League team, 'the claret and gold', whose ground was at Fartown, near the Birkby terminus. Images of team members are shown in the car's lower deck windows. (Author's collection)

──────→ 112. The usual car to be decorated and illuminated for special events in the later decades of the system was UEC car 78. Its first outing in this guise was to celebrate the Victory in 1918. From then it was habitually used to celebrate local and national occasions including the opening of the tramway to Brighouse on 12th March 1923 as seen here, when it operated between Rastrick and Brighouse. The uncanopied BEC car behind was the normal type of tram originally used on this route. (Roy Brook collection)

──────→ 113. Another event when car 78 was decorated was for a road safety campaign as seen here. The final occasion when an illuminated tram operated was to celebrate the Coronation of King George VI in May 1937 and again, this car was used. (Author's collection)

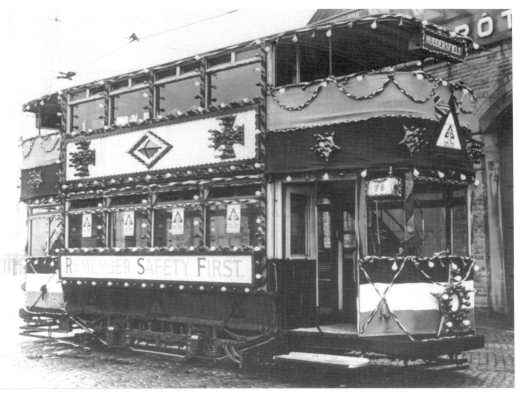

TRAM CREWS

114. The driver and conductor of steam tram engine no 14 and trailer pose with their charge in Lockwood Road. Whilst the conductor is dressed in uniform, the driver, spanner in hand, is less formally attired as befits his working environment of driving and firing (and occasionally uncoupling) the engine. The conductor carries the brass Kaye's Patent fare collector, an early form of fare box, in which passengers deposited their fares. No tickets were issued. (Kirklees Museums and Galleries K008794)

115. The crew of enclosed car 136 during the 1930s. Note the differing styles of uniform. This is possibly a winter scene – in summer white tops were added to the uniform hats. The conductor's equipment includes a whistle and ticket punch which he will use in conjunction with a ticket rack containing the stock of tickets, each fare denomination being of a different colour. (WB Stocks / Kirklees Museums and Galleries K020176)

120. Many of the trams were sold off without mechanical components to serve as sheds, holiday homes and sports pavilions. These could be seen around the town and further afield for many years after the tramway era. One of the last to survive was the lower half of Huddersfield's last tram, car 132, which was placed in a farmer's field near Castle Hill and remained there until the early 1960s. Despite a preservation attempt, this historical relic was broken up and no Huddersfield tram has survived. (Huddersfield Examiner / Kirklees Museums and Galleries Ke15870)

MP Middleton Press

EVOLVING THE ULTIMATE RAIL ENCYCLOPEDIA

Easebourne Lane, Midhurst, West Sussex.
GU29 9AZ Tel:01730 813169

www.middletonpress.co.uk email:info@middletonpress.co.uk

A-0 906520 B-1 873793 C-1 901706 D-1 904474

OOP Out of print at time of printing - Please check availability BROCHURE AVAILABLE SHOWING NEW TITLES